WINDOW
TREATMENTS

WINDOW
TREATMENTS

· · · · · · · · · · · · · · · · · ·

A PRACTICAL GUIDE TO CURTAINS
AND BLINDS FOR YOUR HOME

HEATHER LUKE

MEREHURST

First published in 1995 by Merehurst Limited,
Ferry House, 51-57 Lacy Road, Putney, London SW15 1PR

Copyright © Merehurst Limited 1995

ISBN 1 85391 487 8

A catalogue record of this book is available from
the British Library

Edited by Dulcie Andrews
Designed by Ivor Claydon
Illustrated by Corinne and Ray Burrows
Typesetting by Cameron Typesetting
Colour separation by P&W Graphics, Singapore
Printed in Italy by G. Canale + C. SpA.

ACKNOWLEDGMENTS

Special Photography by Paul Ryder
Styling by Michelle Roberts

Robert Harding Syndication supplied transparencies on pages 1 & 38
by Debi Treloar, Homes & Gardens; pages 2 & 22 by Graham Rae,
Ideal Home; page 3 by Dominic Blackmore, Homes & Ideas;
page 4 (bottom) by Tom Leighton, Homes & Gardens.

Photography on page 11 by Paul Ryan, International Interiors; pages 16
and 57 supplied by Sanderson; page 26 by Brock, Robert Harding Picture
Library; page 33 supplied by Heather Luke & John Freeman.

The publishers would like to thank Laura Ashley plc and
Today Interiors Ltd. for supplying photographs.

Contents

Introduction

Windows are a most important aspect of both room design and building design; they are the 'eyes' of the building and should be designed specifically to balance the whole. Any major alteration in size, configuration and construction has a dramatic effect on the facade. Windows are usually one of the first features noticed from the outside and to which the eye is first drawn once inside. The extreme variations between day and night, wintertime and summertime, make windows an important feature of any room decoration scheme.

Whatever design or construction method is chosen, the basic principles remain; windows must provide almost all of the natural light which enters a house and be in proportion to the room, controlling temperature and light for comfortable and practical living. They must provide adequate insulation and weather proofing, allow ventilation within the frame design, with the ability to open and close when necessary. They should be easy to clean from inside and out and must be architecturally compatible with the exterior.

The 'dressing' of windows has been a major factor in the furnishing of a room for centuries, and windows may be dressed as formally or as informally as taste, fashion and budget allow. Do not forget that care must be taken that a window treatment should be as pleasing from the exterior as it is from the inside; you may long for orange, blue or red curtain linings, but think how these would look from outside!

The period style, height, size and positioning of windows must all play a part in deciding on a window treatment. Tall, slender windows of the early and late Georgian style, with deep reveals and shutters, clearly demand a different approach from small cottage windows or wide, metal-framed ones. It is always a good idea to do a little research into period window treatments to give you ideas on how best to dress them accurately. The effect is worth the effort.

Arched

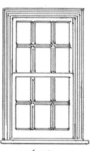

Sash

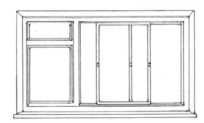

Modern Horizontal

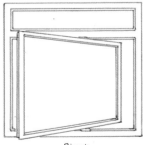

Pivot

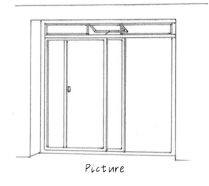

Picture

Dormer

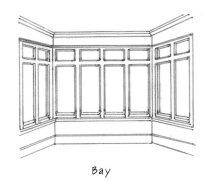

Bay

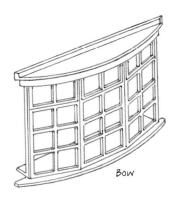

Bow

Casement

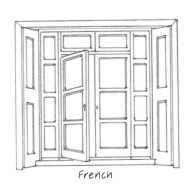

French

A Few General Rules

Whilst some of the best design schemes have come about by breaking all of the rules, this can only be done successfully with great skill and long experience. The amateur should follow a few simple guidelines to produce window treatments which will be guaranteed to work well before venturing into risky areas, which can not only be desperately disappointing but also very costly if serious errors are made. Below are some hints to ensure success.

• Is the window treatment you are considering appropriate? You must ask yourself this question dispassionately, as heart ruling head has spoiled many a good design scheme. You may be desperate to use a favourite fabric; think carefully first. It may, of course, be perfect for curtains - but, more often than not, it can be used more effectively as a cushion or tablecloth, which is designed to take special attention in the room, rather than for the curtains which should form part of the overall framework.

• If the view is wonderful and there is no need for privacy, leave the window uncurtained or treat very simply. I personally dislike the 'black holes' which night time gives and, in some cases, I have devised window hangings which are folded away during the daytime to give a clear view. Try a blind made in a fabric to match the walls, which can be pulled up unobtrusively.

• All windows should be framed by their treatment and should act like a picture frame in drawing the eye to the beyond.

• If the view is really ugly, the window should become the feature. Choose an elaborate drape or a flat blind with a dramatic design, such as a huge bunch of peonies in a Chinese pot, which itself becomes a picture.

• At night, when the curtains are fully drawn, they should not overpower.

• As a general rule, curtaining should tone with the walls rather than contrast.

• Simple, elegant windows need simple, elegant treatments. Avoid large, heavy floral patterns.

Draping for an interesting piece of fabric across a recessed window creates a focal point in a room.

• Use soft plain colours in the drawing room and make use of the wonderful fringes and other trimmings which are so readily available today. Save chintzes for the bedrooms or a sunny morning room.

• Architecturally-strong windows need strong treatments: defined pelmets, Roman blinds, and so on.

Climate and Season

The climate of the country in which you live will, to a certain extent, dictate the type of window treatment and the colours which are suitable. The very heavy drapes which are wonderfully cosy in northern countries feel oppressive in the Mediterranean. In the same

way, lemon yellow can sing in the south and look harsh and uncomfortable in the north.

The filmy white treatments which look so fresh in hot countries look glorious in summer but can appear chilly and dull in a cold winter climate; therefore, as we all love to have the sun streaming into our rooms, many people are now reverting to the old tradition of summer and winter curtains. I often use lightweight under-curtains, which are left hanging all year round, underneath much heavier curtains, which are removed as soon as the temperature allows and re-hung once the evenings start to draw in.

Careful Planning

It is worth taking a little time to decide on the right window treatments when you move into a new house or apartment — better an old sheet pinned up for privacy than an expensive mistake. Think carefully about the most suitable style. For example, if the window is architecturally good and the view wonderful, it might be best to keep the aspect clean and uncluttered by any colour or fabric, perhaps using a simple white muslin drape or shutters to dress the windows in question.

Fabrics

BROCADE
Brocade is traditionally woven using silk, cotton, wool or mixed fibres, on a jacquard loom, in a multi- or self-coloured floral design. Traditional motifs such as cherubs, vases, ribbons, bunches of flowers and so on are mixed together.

CALICO
Named after Calicut in India where it was first introduced, this is a coarse, plain-weave cotton in cream or white with 'natural' flecks.

CHINTZ
Traditionally a cotton fabric with Eastern design using flowers and birds, often with a resin finish which gave a characteristic sheen (glaze) which repels dirt. The term is now used to describe any patterned or plain glazed fabric.

DAMASK
A jacquard first woven in Damascus in silk, wool or cotton with satin floats on a warp satin background, most damasks are self-coloured and can be made up reversed for a matte finish.

DENIM
This fabric is inexpensive and available in many weights, from light chambray to heavy jeans' denim.

GINGHAM
A plain-weave fabric with equal width stripes of white plus one other colour in both warp and weft threads to produce blocks of checks or stripes, gingham is either 100 percent cotton or a cotton mix.

LACE
Open-work fabrics in designs ranging from simple spots to elaborate panels, lace is generally available in cotton or a cotton and polyester mixture.

MOIRE
The characteristic 'watermarked' markings are produced as plain woven silk or acetate fabric progresses through hot, engraved cylinders crushing threads into different directions to form the pattern.

MUSLIN
A white or off-white, open-weave cloth which can be dyed, muslin is inexpensive but should be used with at least triple fullness for floaty bed drapes and as under-curtains to diffuse light.

ORGANDIE
The very finest cotton fabric usually from Switzerland, an acid finish gives organdie a unique crispness.

ORGANZA
Similar to organdie and made of silk, polyester or viscose, organza is very springy and used for stiffened headings of fine fabrics. Its crisp texture allows it to be made up into Roman blinds used to filter light and insects and to protect the main curtains.

SILK NOILE
Light- to medium-weight silk in a natural colour, silk noile features small pieces of the cocoon woven in as flecks.

TAFFETA
Ordinarily woven from silk, taffeta is now available in acetate and blends. A plain-weave fabric with a light-catching sheen resulting from weaving fibres which have a sheen; use for elaborate drapes for its light-reflecting qualities.

VELVET
Originally 100 percent silk, now made from cotton and viscose, care needs to be taken when sewing with velvet or the fabrics will 'walk'. Always buy a good velvet with a dense pile which will not pull out easily, and always press on a pin board.

VOILE
Fine, light plain-weave cotton or polyester fabric dyed in many plain colours, silk and wool voiles can be used for fine drapery.

Measuring Windows

Obstructions

First of all, look for anything around the window which might influence the position of the curtain fitting: pipes, electrical sockets, electrical cables, radiator thermostats - in short, anything which would be better hidden behind the curtains should be taken into consideration. Check the run of electrical wires which could prevent fixing into a particular spot.

Making Templates

When measuring, make templates around anything that might be in the way so that the headings of curtains or pelmets can be shaped around the obstacle if necessary and the fittings can be adjusted to take care of any interruptions. Use brown paper and tape to the edges of the window. Draw around the obstruction if possible. If not, tear the paper roughly and cut in accurately with a sharp knife.

Unsightly Fittings

Stand back and look at the window, checking for any ugly fittings which might need to be covered. Measure and note the positions of ugly double-glazing

fittings, blind fittings, odd bits of wood and so on. Decide whether you need blinds and/or pelmets or fixed curtain headings to cover these. Plan exactly how and where they should be positioned.

Accurate Measurements

Take at least three measurements across the window so that you are aware of any unevenness. Curtain fixings must always be level, so you might need to use a spirit level when measuring if the ceiling, window or floor slope in different directions.

A window frame width
B window frame height
C recess width
D recess height
E sill width
F ceiling to top of window frame or recess
G ceiling to floor
H under sill to floor
I to the next obstruction

The sheer delight of this window treatment owes its success to careful planning.

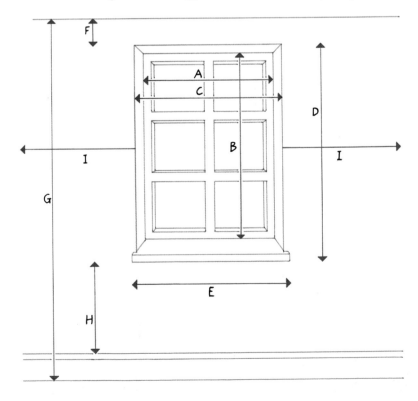

Estimating Fabric

Before you can work out the fabric quantity you will need to buy, you must establish the style of your window treatment following the ideas on pages 14-15. Take the measurements of the pole width, the stack back, the hook drop and the overall drop.

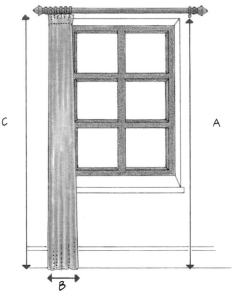

A = hook drop
B = stack back
C = overall drop

To estimate quantities you do not need exact measurements; these will be taken before making up, once the fittings are in place.

1 To work out the cut lengths, add both heading and hem allowances to the hook drop or the overall drop referring to the Quick Reference Chart (opposite). For my example, I will only use centimetres to avoid confusion.

Say, 215 + 16 + 16 = 247cm. So each cut of fabric will be 247cm.

2 To work out how many cuts you need, take the fitting length and divide in half for each curtain. Multiply by the fullness required. Add 5cm (2 in) for the centre overlap, 8cm (3 ¼ in) for the return and 12cm (4 ¾ in) for the side turnings.
Say, the pole is 140cm.
140 ÷ 2 = 70cm x 2.5 = 175cm.
Add 5 + 8 + 12 = 200cm.
Divide this figure by the width of your curtain fabric,
say, 130cm, therefore
200cm ÷ 130 = 1.53cm.
You will need one-and-a-half widths of fabric for each curtain.
Each cut is 247cm and you will need three cuts:
247 x 3 = 741cm, say 7.5m.

3 If your fabric has a pattern, each cut will need to fit within complete pattern repeats.
For example, if the pattern repeat is 65cm you will need four complete pattern repeats for each cut. 4 x 65 = 260cm.
So the total amount of fabric needed will be increased to:

3 x 260 = 780cm, say 8m.
It is advisable always to buy an extra complete pattern repeat so that you can plan your first cut - the part of the pattern which you wish to see at heading and hem.

Make a note of the wastage which will occur. It might be enough to make a bed valance or some cushions. In this example, each cut was 247cm so there would be 13cm wastage from each cut. Not enough for anything much - but perhaps covered coat hangers, or frills to edge two cushions.

4 Blinds will be worked out following the same method and the Quick Reference Chart.

Cutting Hints

In a large piece of fabric there are almost bound to be flaws, so it is important to check the whole piece carefully before you start. If flaws or marks are minor, plan your cuts around them as far as possible.

Ideally, the pattern should be printed exactly following the grain of the fabric but, unfortunately, this is only the case in the very best fabrics. If it 'goes off' by more than 2cm (¾ in), you will need to decide whether to keep the fabric or whether to return it.

Fabric should be cut square to the selvedge and also as nearly as possible to the pattern. Make sure that the pattern matches equally at the eye-line where the left and right curtains will meet. Mark the front and top of all cuts of plain fabric with a coloured tack on the right-hand side. Selvedge writing on a printed cloth will need to be cut away - you want to prevent the possibility of being able to read the manufacturer's name through the curtains. Snip into the selvedges of woven fabrics to allow the seams to react to atmospheric changes with the rest of the curtain.

Using your estimating plan, measure and mark with pins all the cuts required on to the piece of fabric. When you are satisfied that you have planned correctly, measure again and then cut. Leave pieces flat overnight to stabilize.

Always measure twice and cut once!

QUICK REFERENCE CHART

Headings

flat headings	8cm (3 ¼ in) to hook drop
gathered tape for pole or track	16cm (6 ⅜ in) to hook drop
gathered tape under pelmet board	6cm (2 ⅜ in) to hook drop
pencil pleat tape	8cm (3 ¼ in) to hook drop
ruched on to 35mm (1 ½ in) pole	20cm (8 in) to hook drop
pocket heading for wires, voiles	12cm (4 ¾ in) to hook drop
French pleats, goblets & inverted pleats 10cm (4 in) deep	18cm (7 ¼ in) to overall drop
French pleats, goblets & inverted pleats 15cm (6 in) deep	28cm (11 ¼ in) to overall drop

Hems

unlined curtain	16cm (6 ⅜ in)
lined curtain	16cm (6 ⅜ in)
interlined curtain	11cm (4 ⅜ in)
bound hem	none

Fullness allowance

flat headings	1 - 2
gathered headings	1.5 - 3
pencil pleat	2.5 - 3
ruched headings	2 - 2.5
voiles	3 - 3.5
bunched	2 - 3
French pleats	2.5 - 3
goblets	2 - 3
inverted pleats	2 - 2.5

Blinds

Roman	none
Cascade	5cm (2 in) per width
Rolled	4cm (1 ½ in) per width
London	12-20cm (4 ¾-8 in) per pleat
Austrian	1.5 - 2.5 widths

Planning the Treatment

There are so many ideas and styles for window treatments that it can be difficult to judge which would best suit your particular furnishings, home and window. Making a mistake may not only be financially disastrous but will be distressing and a waste of valuable time. We are all by nature creative, we all have our own individual style and there is now everything available which we could possibly need to interpret that style. So often, however, due to of lack of self-confidence, we tend to play safe to the detriment of our creative abilities and our homes. Never be afraid to make a mistake; it is in making mistakes that we learn, and nothing can ever be a complete disaster - the very worst curtains can be made into a bedcover, cushions, or used as lining.

The easiest and safest way to experiment with ideas for your window treatment is with paper and pen. I meet many people who are paralysed by the thought of drawing - but I have not met a single person who is not totally surprised at their own capabilities within one hour. This method is the simplest possible with the fewest measurements.

You will need graph paper, tracing paper, a good pencil or drawing pen and a ruler. Firstly, transfer your window measurements on to paper. You are only experimenting with ideas so round figures up or down to make life easier. You only need the outside frame height and width, plus the floor to ceiling measurement. Choose a scale which is easy and works with your paper - say 1 - 20. Therefore each cm of graph paper will be equal to 20cm of room measurement. Once you have decided on your scale, you are ready to begin:

• Draw the basic window and room height on your graph paper. Add a skirting line to make the proportion a little more realistic.

• Place a piece of tracing paper over and hold with paper clips. Experiment with different window treatments. Take ideas from magazines, but start simply.

• A pole fitted just above the window but one-third of the window wider on each side will allow the maximum light into the room. The window will look wider and shorter.

• A pole fitted at a higher level and hardly wider than the window will allow less light in but will make the window look taller, narrower and more elegant.

• Short curtains tied back at a high level give a country – cottage feel to this same window.

• Try a swagged pelmet and curtains draped back in the traditional position and you will hardly believe you are dressing the same window.

None of the above ideas is right or wrong. Each has its own place. Window dressing can transform a room but should always work with your furnishings. The right treatment can also be used to balance an odd window.

Unlined Curtains

Unlined curtains are the simplest form of window covering to make. If you are unsure of your skills or are tackling home furnishings for the first time, this is a good place to start.

Preparation

Estimate the number of widths of fabric you will need for each curtain (very fine fabrics should be three times fullness). Calculate the finished drop and add 16cm (6 ¾ in) for the hem plus the allowance for your chosen heading.

Making Up

1 Cut out the lengths. Trim away selvedges and any writing on the seam. Join widths with a French seam.

2 Working on a flat surface, turn in both side edges 6cm (2 ⅜ in) to the wrong side. Press. Re-open the turnings and fold in half to give 3cm (1 ¼ in) turnings. Pin and press. Turn up the hem 16cm (6 ¾ in). Press. Re-open and fold in half as before. Pin and press.

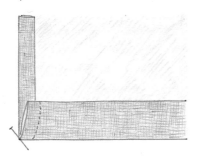

3 To mitre the corner:
a) Position a temporary pin exactly through the point of the corner.
b) Open out all folds and fold the corner inwards level with the pin. Re-fold so that the inside folds of both side and hem turnings will meet to form an angled mitre. Press lightly.

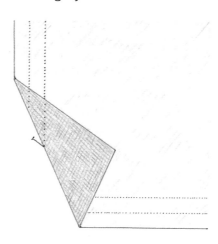

c) Re-fold the sides and hem along the pressed lines. Make sure that the pin is still on the point and the fabric is lying flat inside. Pin and press.

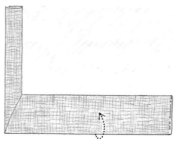

4 Neatly slip stitch both sides and hem, inserting a fabric weight at each corner and seam. Stitch the mitre with tiny neat ladder stitches.

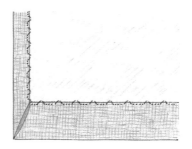

5 Lie the curtain on a flat surface, wrong side up, making sure that there are no creases in the fabric. From the hem, using a long ruler, measure your finished drop and mark with a pin. Repeat this six times across each width of fabric. Mark this line with a tacking thread and make your chosen heading.

Lined Curtains

You will need a flat surface to work on when making these. The extra layer of fabric gives more body to the main fabric, protects the main fabric from sunlight and adds insulation.

1 Estimate and cut out your fabric and lining. Join widths of fabric, press seams open and trim away selvedges neatly. Join lining and press seams open. Turn the lining hem up 10cm (4 in) and press. Fold in half to give a 5cm (2 in) hem. Pin and slip stitch. Press and put to one side.

2 Lay the curtain fabric on your worktable, wrong side up. Press thoroughly to remove any creases. Fold over the sides 6cm (2 ⅜ in) each, pin and press. Turn up the hem 16cm (6 ¾ in), ensure that the pattern runs evenly across the width, and press. Open out the hem line fold and re-fold in half to make an 8cm (3 ¼ in) double hem. Pin and press.

3 To mitre the corners:
a) Position a temporary pin exactly through the point of the corner.

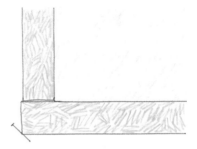

b) Open out the folds and turn in the corner so that the pin is visible.

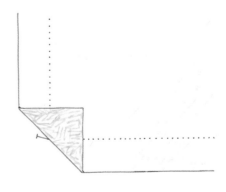

The addition of a contrasting fabric as a lining can create a very stylish effect. Here, the emphasis is on colour and texture, using fabrics which complement each other beautifully.

c) Re-fold the sides and hems and mitre the corner so that the side and hem turnings line up. Keep the pin on the point. Pin and press.

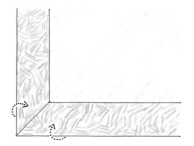

4 Herringbone stitch down both sides of the curtain, making stitches approximately 3cm (1¼ in). Picking up only one thread at a time, loosely slip stitch the hem. Insert a weight in each seam. Slip a weight into each corner and ladder stitch both mitres.

5 Using the pre-prepared curtain lining, place it on top of curtain, wrong sides together. Match the seams exactly and position the lining so that the top of the lining hem lines up with the top of the curtain hem. Turn back the lining and lock-in (page 61) twice across the width at equal distances and also on any seams, using the same colour thread as the main fabric.

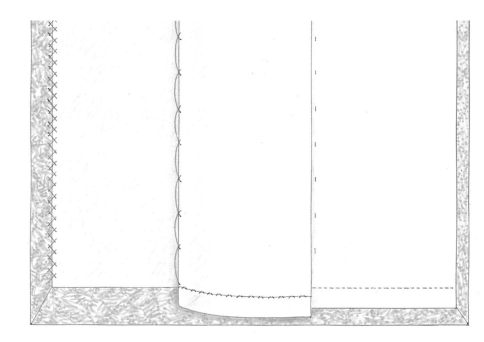

6 Reposition the lining and smooth out. Trim away any excess lining from each side of the curtain. Turn in the edges of the lining 3cm (1¼ in) and pin. Neatly stitch down the edges of the curtain, beginning about 4cm (1½ in) around the bottom corner and continuing until just below the heading.

7 From the hem of the curtain, measure the overall drop and place a marking pin. Measure six times across each width of fabric. Mark this line with tacking thread and make your chosen heading.

17

Curtain Headings

Hand-pleated Headings

Hand-pleated headings are made using stiff buckram. The most useful widths are either 10 or 15cm (4 or 6 in). The curtain fabric will fold over the buckram and back under again. If 10cm (4 in) buckram is being used, 18cm (7 ¼ in) extra fabric to the overall drop of the curtain should be allowed. If 15cm (6 in) buckram is being used, 28cm (11 ¼ in) extra fabric to the overall drop of the curtain should be allowed.

1 Fold back the lining along the tack line. Cut away interlining along this line. Fold the lining back up. Set the buckram on to the curtain so that the top of it lies on the pinned and pressed line. Trim so that it finishes 2cm (¾ in) in from each side. Refold curtain over buckram and tuck edges underneath. Neatly fold both ends of fabric under.

2 Make a heading pleat plan, including the overlap, the pleats, the gaps and the return across the width. Fold and pin pleats firmly in position at the top and bottom of buckram.

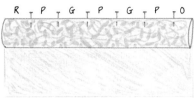

3 Machine down the length of the buckram and fasten securely. Slip stitch the sides down from the top of the curtain and along to the first pleat.

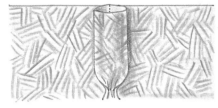

FRENCH PLEATS: To turn the pleats into triple French pleats, place three fingers in pleat and flatten. Lift the pleat and pinch in the centre fold. Push down to make three equal pleats. At the base of the pleat, 12mm (½ in) below the buckram, stitch through the three pleats. At the top of the pleat stitch each piece in position so that it holds its shape.

GOBLETS: To turn the pleats into goblet pleats, simply open the stitched pleat out with your fingers and run a gathering thread around the base of the pleat, 12mm (½ in) below the base of the buckram. Stuff the goblet pleat with rolls of interlining, to give a good, rounded shape.

Gathered Headings

USING TAPES: A gathered heading is easily achieved by stitching a bought tape at the hook drop measurement with extra fabric above to make a frill. The frill can be any size from 2 to 8cm (⅜ to 3 ½ in). The former is suitable for a track under a pelmet, and the latter can be used to cover a track or pole completely. Any deeper and the frill will become floppy. Allow 6cm (2 ⅜ in) for a frilled heading with a pole.

The standard heading tape is 2.5cm (l in) deep. Decide on the size of the heading frill and allowing double; measure from the marked hook drop to the end of the heading allowance. Trim any excess. Fold the heading allowance in half and pin the heading tape in position. Stitch in place. Pull up to the required width.

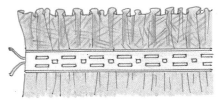

FOR A DEEP FRILL: Following the same method, a very deep frill can be made to deliberately flop over. Make up to 25cm (10 in) - doubled over, so allow 50cm (20 in) - and stiffen inside slightly. Allow double to two-and-a-half times fullness

BUNCHED HEADINGS: These are also made in this way. Allow 30cm (12 in) - doubled over, so allow 60cm (24 in) - and stitch ordinary tape along the hook drop line. Pull up and fasten. Holding the fabric in both hands, pull the fold apart and towards the front to cover the tape stitching lines, at the same time 'bunching' the fabric with your fingers. Using a long thread and random stitches, catch the heading in place, through to the back. Allow two-and-a-half to three times fullness

POCKET OR CHANNELED HEADING: This is a very easy form of heading for voiles and to ruche curtains over a pole. Unless the pocket is very large, the curtains will not be able to pull and will need to be tied back.

Measure the circumference of the pole and add an easement allowance of at least 20 percent; half of this measurement will be the pocket size. Allow 2cm (¾ in) for voiles and 7cm (2 ¾ in) for a 35mm (1 ½ in) pole. The frill above the heading is adjustable but, as a general guide, 2cm (¾ in) for voiles and 7cm (2 ¾ in) for curtains. The fabric will be folded back with a hem allowance for heavier fabric and three times for lightweights; so, for voiles allow 12cm (4 ¾ in) above the hook drop and, for curtains with a 35mm (1 ½ in) pole, allow 20cm (8 in).

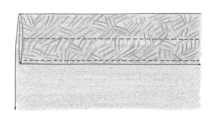

Flat Headings

Some of the more striking fabrics, especially those with a strong pictorial scene, really look better not gathered. Flat headings work with curtains of up to one-and-two-thirds fullness.

Add 8cm (3 ½ in) to your hook drop. Fold fabric to the wrong side and fold under to give a 4cm (1 ½ in) turning. Stitch 6mm (¼ in) from both fold lines.

1 Pin lengths of ribbon at intervals of approximately 16cm (3 ⅜ in) and stitch to the heading following the first stitching lines.

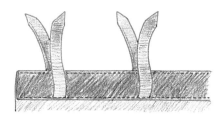

2 Make holes with a punch and rivet set, obtainable from stationery suppliers. Thread the curtain on to a pole, or thread cord, string or ribbon through these holes and tie on to the pole.

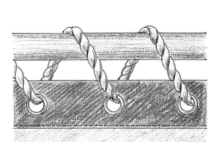

3 Fix hooks or wooden pegs to the door or window frame and hook the curtain heading on.

Tie-backs

Tie-backs are necessary when curtains must remain pulled back to allow more light into a room or when a curtain hangs by a doorway and may keep blowing out when the door is open; however, they are mainly used for decorative purposes. Long, tall windows need tie-backs positioned one-third up from the floor; smaller windows can be given a totally different look if tied back two-thirds up. Fabric can be used in numerous ways – matched to the curtain, three complementary fabrics plaited together, two contrasting fabric rolls twisted together, sashes made short to tie into neat bows or long and flowing with huge bows - but care must be taken to choose a fabric and style to work with the window treatment.

Cut a template of the tie-back you have in mind in calico and hold around the curtain, making sure that the curtain will be able to drape without the leading edges becoming creased - tie-backs should hold the curtain back in a lovely sweep. Pull the curtains slightly and lift just the first two or three folds so that a soft drape is made. The tie-back should hold this shape so that the drape will not fall out, but also so that the leading edges do not become horribly creased. If you have chosen several layers of curtaining or mixed curtaining and blinds for your window treatment, you might keep the outside pair permanently tied back. In this case, tighten the tie-back so that the curtain drape becomes fuller and permanently held.

Shaped Piped Tie-back

Materials

- small piece of pelmet buckram
- main fabric
- flanged cord or piping cord to go around each tie-back
- small piece interlining
- 2 x 20mm (¾ in) brass rings

1 Cut two pieces of main fabric to your template, adding a 1.5cm (⅝ in) seam allowance all around. Cut one piece of pelmet buckram and one piece of interlining to the template size. You could use double thickness of heading buckram if you do not have access to pelmet buckram.

2 Pin the interlining to the tie-back front. Pin the piped or flanged cord all around with the stitching line on the seam allowance. Snip into the stitching line every 1.5cm (⅝ in) for a good fit. Join the cord ends on the side which will be behind the curtain. Stitch in place, as close to the piping cord as possible. Trim interlining back to the seam line and snip V-cuts into the seam allowance to make sure that the piping lies flat. Press seam inwards. Fit the buckram inside, against the interlining and under the seam.

3 Press the seam allowance under all around the back piece. Pin to the piping line on the tie-back and slip stitch to the piping stitching line, using very small stitches so that the stitches do not gape when the tie-back is curved around the curtain. Stitch one brass ring on the back right at the end and one far enough in not to show from the front.

These tie-backs can be made in many different shapes - experiment with calico or paper. You could stitch ribbons at each end to tie, decorate with ribbon or contrast binding, add a frill or fringing to the lower edge, or pin fresh flowers on for a special occasion.

Plaited Tie-back

These tie-backs are soft so can be made tighter than the harder, shaped type. Three rolls of 12cm (4 ¾ in) make a finished tie-back width of approximately 7cm (2 ¾ in).

Materials

- 3 strips of fabric twice the length of the finished tie-back x 12cm (4¾ in)
- 3 pieces of 2oz polyester wadding, 40cm (16in) x length of fabric
- 2 x 20mm (¾ in) brass rings

1 Roll the pieces of wadding to the required diameter and herringbone stitch along the raw edge to hold. Press in 1.5cm (⅝ in) on one side of each of the main fabric strips along the length. Place each of the rolls on to the strips. Fold the strips over the rolls and pin the folded edge over the raw edge along the length. Slip stitch.

2 Pin the three pieces to the worktable with the ends close together and plait. Cut two 4cm (1 ½ in) squares of the main fabric. Press under 12mm (½ in) on all sides. Hold the ends together and stitch the squares over the raw edges. Stitch brass rings to the back of each end.

Finish with a rosette, a bow or silk flowers. Use three different coloured fabrics or mix floral checks and stripes.

Bows and Sashes

A simple sash can be used in many ways: formally with a contrast edging and knotted like a tie, or very full and several metres long - it could be draped around the curtain several times, finishing with a huge bow or soft knot. Experiment with a scarf or piece of calico.

Materials

- main fabric
- 2 x 20mm (¾ in) brass rings

1 Cut one piece of fabric the length and double the chosen width, allowing 1.5cm (⅝ in) seam allowances. Fold in half lengthways, right side inside, and pin. Trim the two ends to an angle of 45 degrees. Stitch from each end to within 5cm (2 in) of the middle. Trim seam to 12 mm (½ in) and snip across the corners. Pull through the gap. Press seams flat. Use a pin to pull the last bit of fabric through and make sharp corners.

2 Tie the sash around the curtain to decide where the bow or knot should be. Mark the place where the sash meets the tie-back hook. Cut in half to make two pieces. Fold the raw edges under and run a gathering thread through. Stitch small rings to the inside so that they cannot be seen from the front.

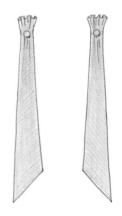

Curtain Tracks & Poles

There are so many tracks available, it is sometimes difficult to know which to buy. Metal tracks with plastic runners (less noisy than metal runners) and a pull-cord system wholly enclosed within the track are the most reliable, uncomplicated to fit and are available in several different qualities to suit the weight and length of your curtains. Fittings are adaptable to 'top fit' on to a pelmet board, or into a recess, or to 'face fit' to the wall, to a batten or into the window frame.

Lightweight Curtains

Most sheers are fitted into the recess or behind the main curtain track or pole, so fittings need to be as invisible as possible. Choose between tiny metal tracks which will top fix with pin nails or clear plastic tracks which will adapt to top or face fix.

Specific Use

Arched windows need special tracks to hold the curtains in place at close intervals against the wall, either inside or on the front of the recess. These tracks are formed with very small sections of metal with a hole for the curtain hook, pivoted together so that they will sleeve inside each other to a greater or lesser extent, depending on the angle of the curve.

Bay Windows

Metal tracks in any weight can be bent to fit around a bay window, whether three-, five- or seven-sided, or semi-circular.

Left: The white pole is perfect for this simple Swedish country-style window treatment. A white pole with finial sat each end is the correct fitting in this situation. Opposite page: A curled end to an iron pole adds visual interest.

Cording

Cording is essential to keep curtains in good condition. When curtains are pulled by hand they will inevitably become marked on the leading edges. The best cording sets are enclosed within the track to prevent the curtain hooks catching the cords and jamming the system. The cords can be cut and weighted with a brass S-clip slipped on to prevent the cords twisting together.

Fitting the Track

Tracks can be fitted to the wall - 'face fixed' - or to the ceiling - 'top fixed'. Most fittings are adaptable for both uses. Always drill a hole large enough and long enough to ensure that the fitting is secure. The packaged tracks will generally include the appropriate screws and plugs. The side fittings which hold the track to the wall are available in several different sizes so that the track can be fitted either very close to the wall or some distance out. This facility allows the curtains to hang straight over a radiator or deep sill. A deeper fitting also allows space for a blind to fit in behind the curtains, or for two pairs of curtains to hang from one fitting. Use centre fittings as often as is recommended on the instructions.
NOTE: Remember always to use a spirit level.

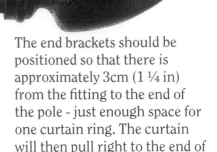

Choosing Your Pole

So many variations of pole finishes and finial style are available that the possibilities for interesting combinations are endless. You may choose a cherry wood pole with an ebony line for a Grecian look, or a chunky pole with a country-style paint finish for a rustic look - or any number of styles in between. In every situation, poles should be chosen with a diameter and a finial style which suits both the room and the planned curtain design. A long, heavy curtain will need a chunky, solid pole and proportionate finials; a small cottage window will need a much smaller pole. Poles fall into several categories.

WOOD - stained to any finish.

BRASS - use only solid brass and finials. Brass poles are available from tiny 12mm (½ in) diameter for use on wardrobe doors with ruched fabric or inside the smallest window, to chunky 10cm (4 in) diameter poles which will carry the longest, heaviest curtains.

BRASS AND WOOD - mix both, for example dark mahogany pole with brass finials and rings.

METAL - 12-30mm (½-1 ¼ in) in diameter, metal (steel) poles can be bent or finished to size and painted any colour. Matte spray paint is easiest to use. Many shapes of finials available: balls, ovals, spearheads, baskets, and rams horns.

PAINTED WOOD - water-based paints can be rubbed into light wood poles to add a touch of colour. They should be varnished with an acrylic varnish to help the rings slide.

Fitting the pole

Position poles with the balance of the window in mind. If in doubt, 10cm (4 in) above the reveal and 15-20cm (6-8 in) to either side is a safe guide. Pole treatments can look extremely unattractive if the curtains have to stretch too far over the window to find the end of the pole.

The end brackets should be positioned so that there is approximately 3cm (1 ¼ in) from the fitting to the end of the pole - just enough space for one curtain ring. The curtain will then pull right to the end of the pole and fill the available stack-back space.

Cording

Poles can be bought with pull cords which run smoothly in metal channels housed into the top of the pole, preventing too much handling of the leading edges of the curtains. Overlap arms in metal are also available which allow the curtains to close completely and overlap neatly. The only way to 'cord' antique poles is to tie a cord to the leading ring and thread through eyes fitted to the wall behind the pole.

Swing arms

Poles on swing arms can be used to fit inside dormer windows. The curtains must be made either with the main fabric on both sides or with one fabric on one side and a contrasting fabric on the opposite side, as both sides will be equally visible. The headings will ruche on to the pole and be kept in place with a ball finial. The arms swing across the window at night and open on to the side walls during the daytime.

Blinds

The batten should have a screw eye fitted at the top of each cord and a china thimble or large screw eyes at the side which the blind will be pulled. Fit the batten to the window frame or into the wall and fit the cleat within easy reach.

Thread each cord through the screw eyes, starting at the side with one cord and passing it through all the screw eyes and the cord carrier. Work along the blind, passing each cord through the screw eye in line with each row and through each screw eye towards the end of the batten until all cords are through the carrier. Holding all cords firmly, pull the blind up and down several times. Look behind to check that cords are not twisted or caught up, then cut the cords evenly. Thread the cord weight through and knot securely to make sure that the cords cannot pull back through.

It is best to use a cord joiner if there are several cords. With the blind down, cut the cord approximately 5cm (2 in) from the thimble and knot inside one half of the cord joiner. Thread a single cord through the other side and knot securely. Screw the cord joiner together and fit a weight to the end of the single cord.

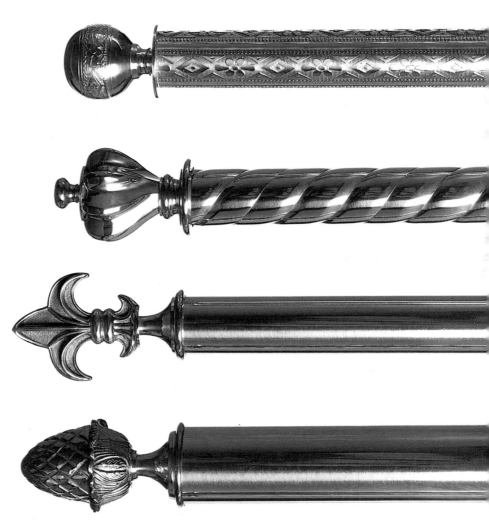

Section two

The Projects

Project 1:
· · · · · · · · · ·

An Austrian Blind for a Long, Tall Window

Long, tall windows are usually architect-designed to be a special feature of the house or apartment but, unfortunately, can also be the unhappy result of an amateur project. Properly planned tall windows will be well balanced to the size of the room and suitably positioned but will dictate a certain strength to the style of decoration. The dilemma imposed by these windows occurs when you realise that any form of window dressing will detract from the architectural strength of both window and room, yet some degree of privacy and protection from sunlight is necessary for day-to-day living.

Any form of blind fitted into the recess will allow the structure to remain the prime factor and will allow complete control of sunlight, provide privacy and cover the 'black hole' of darkness at night time. Roman and rolled blinds, however, are both economical with fabric and straightforward to make. Detail can be added in a restrained or flamboyant way: a stencilled design, contrast bound edges, striped edges and ties, or a fringed and tasselled lower edge.

For a more feminine touch, make a billowy Austrian blind using lightweight, neutral or pastel-coloured silks or cottons. A two-toned silk or a fabric with an embossed weave will add an extra dimension.

Below: The trim on this blind is chosen to match the colour of the wall. Opposite page: The fabric blind is a suitable treatment for this long and tall window.

Project 1: *An Austrian Blind for a Long, Tall Window*
• • • • • • • • • •

Austrian blinds are, more correctly, 'pull-up' curtains. Made up in the same manner as curtains, they may also be unlined, lined or interlined. The addition of rings and cords to the back allow the 'curtain' to be pulled up.

Plan the style and fullness of your blind to suit your window. Using blue-tack or masking tape, secure a piece of string to one side of the window at the top and drape across to the other side, fixing the string into scallop shapes where you think the scallops should eventually be. An uneven number of scallops will usually look better than an even number. Stand back and check that your ideas are right.

To estimate the fabric needed, measure the length of string and add 20cm (8 in) allowance for side turnings. Divide this figure by the width of your fabric to find the number of cuts needed. For example (I will use only centimetres in this example to keep it simple):

window width 130cm, including scallops 200cm
200 -:- 130 = 1.69cm
So, two widths of fabric are required. Measure the length of the blind from the top of the batten to the sill plus approximately 30cm (12 in) so that the blind will still have a scalloped shape when down. Add another 10cm (4 in) for the heading. For example,

window length 200cm
 200 + 10 + 30 = 240cm
So, each cut will be 240cm
Total fabric required: 240cm x 2 = 4.8m.

If the blind is to fall to the floor, it usually looks best hanging as a curtain, so the scallop allowance will not be necessary.

Materials
- main fabric as estimated
- lining, same quantity as for main fabric
- heading tape
- blind cord.
- 12mm (½ in) solid brass rings (clear plastic rings can be used but will become brittle and yellow with sunlight)
- Velcro, twin piece the length of the batten
- blind fitting kit

1 Cut fabric lengths and join widths together so that there are no centre seams (for example, ½ width - full width - ½ width). Cut down both sides of the fabric to the width needed. Cut and join the lining in the same manner. Trim selvedges.

2 Place the blind fabric right side down on the worktable and fold over the sides and hems 10cm (4 in). Pin in place. Mitre the bottom corners following the instructions on page 16. Herringbone stitch all around, with stitches approximately 2cm (¾ in) apart. Place the lining on the blind fabric, matching seams carefully, and lock stitch the seams together.

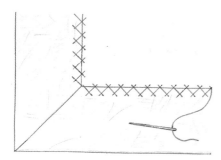

3 Fold the lining sides and hem over so that 7cm (2 ¾ in) of the blind fabric is visible and trim along this fold line. Turn under 1.5cm (⅝ in) all around. Pin and slip stitch in place. Press lightly

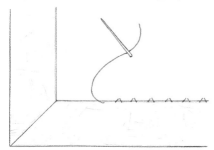

4 Measuring from the bottom up, at 30cm (12 in) intervals across the blind, mark the required finished length with pins. Trim away any excess fabric to 6cm (2 ⅜ in) above the pin line. Fold the fabric and lining over to the lining side, removing pins as you go. Press lightly and pin the heading tape in place.

5 Whilst the blind is still flat on the table, mark the ring positions. Always measure each ring position from the bottom to avoid error. The outside rows should be on the lining edge, and the rest will be divided into the scallops you planned on the window. The spacing of the rings will depend on the length of the blind and how tight you want the fold. Use 20cm (8 in) as a guide.

Stitch each ring in position. The rings must be very secure or they will fall off with use. The stitching should be worked mainly in to the lining to avoid making an ugly mark on the front of the blind. Stitch into the lining three or four times. Stitch through into the main fabric once. Stitch twice more into the lining. Twist the cotton around the stitched threads several times. Fasten off with a double stitch into the threads.

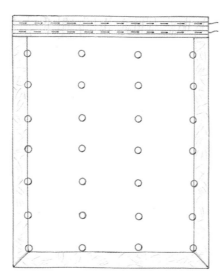

6 Use a sewing machine to attach the heading tape. Always start stitching from the same side, or the fabric will pull and ruckle up on the front. Pull up to the finished width and tie the ends securely.

Cut a strip of lining to the size of the finished blind plus 4cm (1 ½ in) turnings x twice the depth of the tape. Pin the Velcro to the centre of this strip and machine stitch in position. Press the 2cm (¾ in) turnings under at each end and the top and bottom under so that the strip is now the same depth as the heading tape. Hand stitch to the top and bottom of the tape, keeping gathers even.

7 Tie a length of blind cord to the bottom ring and then thread through the rings to the top. Allow each cord to go across the top of the blind and down the other side to the hem. Cut off and repeat with the other cords so that all cords are even. Stitch the cords together at each bottom ring to secure.

8 Cover the batten with the main fabric. Staple the other side of the Velcro to the front and sides. Fit the blind to the batten. Turn over and fit screw eyes into the batten at the top of each row of rings, and a cord carrier at the end with the cords.

Finishing Ideas
• fringed lower edge: stitch fringe to the front of the blind at step 5.
• frilled lower edge: make up a frill of fabric and machine to the lower edge at step 1.

Project 2:
• • • • • • • • • •

Curtains for Recessed Windows

These are mostly found in old houses where a window has been fitted into a very thick wall. Dormer windows are created when a loft in a home or barn has been converted for domestic use - usually a guest bedroom or children's bedrooms and bathrooms. The very nature of the room and the often exposed beams gives a cottagey atmosphere and dictates a simple window treatment.

Both recessed casement and dormer windows always leave a deep recess. If there is a low sill, it could be made into a window seat or, in the case of a full length recess, a storage space can be made under a window seat.

As these windows are frequently small, care should be taken so the window treatment does not dominate or take away valuable light. The window may open outwards or inwards and will need to be dressed accordingly. When the windows have been made to open inwards, the sill is rendered useless unless it cleared every time the window is opened. If there is enough room for the curtains to stack to either side, sill- or floor-length curtains can be hung outside the recess on a decorative pole. Pelmets are usually too overpowering and should be avoided.

Dormer windows usually have recesses which are deeper at the top of the window than the bottom, especially if the window is set high. In this case, the curtain should be caught back to the side into an arm or the bar held back with clips to keep the fitting against the recess during the daytime.

If there is no need to cover the window for privacy, a decorative piece of cotton or lace could be pinned against the window Scandinavian-style and the window seat piled with comfortable cushions.

Blinds can be fitted against the window. Roman or cascade blinds are most suitable, as they have the ability to control the light and add insulation but will fold away neatly without taking more light than necessary on a dull day.

If the depth of the recess is more than half of the window width, curtains can be hung very effectively on swing arms which lie against the recess when opened, allowing maximum light into the room during daytime and covering the window at night. Fabric may be flat or ruched and can be different on opposite sides. Ruched curtains can be caught with a tie-back fixed to the side of the wall to prevent the fabric blowing out of the window with a summer breeze.

Opposite page: Bright and cheerful flower pots feature strongly in this swing-arm window treatment for a deep recessed window in a bathroom. The resulting effect is charming and practical as these can be taken from the frame and cleaned.

Project 2: *Curtains for Recessed Windows*

Swing-frame treatment

Because the shower is to the left of the window and the bath to the right, curtains or blinds fitted to the front of the recess were considered impractical. With a country view and no-one overlooking this window, it was possible to keep the window glass clear; thereby receiving maximum light during the daytime. The strong colours of the sanitary ware and tiles precluded a dainty treatment, so these swing frames were designed as the ideal method to hold fabric flat. During the day time they sit against the recess wall and at night cover the window frame exactly. The idea of using completely different fabrics on either side gave an added dimension to the room.

Measure the recess carefully several times across the width and height. Use a spirit level or set square to check how square the frame is; if your frame is very out of true, use only a top arm and catch the fabric back on the bottom with eyelets and hooks or small clips. Fit the two pairs of arms so that they are exactly perpendicular or the curtains will drop. Take these measurements to your carpenter or local iron worker if you would like to have a solid frame.

Measure the overall drop and width needed for the flat curtains after the frame has been fitted, making no allowance for seams, headings or hems.

Materials

- fabric for the fronts and backs
- 1m (40 in) contrast fabric to bind all around
- 2 swing arms
- 8 buttons, 2cm (¾ in) diameter

1 Cut two rectangles of each fabric to the exact measurements of the finished curtains. Place one on top of the other, wrong sides together. Tack all around using back stitches to prevent movement.

2 Cut four strips of contrast fabric the length of the curtain and 6.5cm (2 ½ in) wide. Take the first strip and place along the edge of one curtain with the cut edges together. Pin across the binding. Machine stitch carefully exactly 1.5cm (⅝ in) in from the cut sides. Repeat with the other three pieces.

3 Press the edgings from the front, away from the curtain. Fold under and pin. Turn curtain to the other side and fold the binding in half to make a 1.5cm (⅝ in) hem on this side also. Pin. Slip stitch into the machined stitches, using very small stitches, so that the binding lies very flat. Repeat with the other three sides.

4 Cut four more strips of the contrast fabric, each the width of the top of the curtain plus 4cm (1 ½ in) for side turnings x 6.5cm (2 ½ in) wide. Place the strips along the tops and bottoms of the curtains. Stitch, press and hem as for the sides, folding the side turning allowance under to hide all raw edges.

5 Cut sixteen strips of fabric 22 x 8cm (8 ¾ x 3 ¾ in). Press each in half lengthways and in half again. Fold under both raw ends and stitch all around, close to the folds.

6 Stitch four of the ties to the front of each curtain, approximately 12cm (4 ¾ in) in from either side and as near to the binding as possible. On the back of each curtain attach four of the strips with the buttons, stitching firmly in place. Tie on to the bars with the ties knotted at the front.

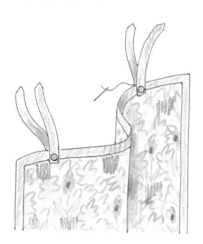

OTHER OPTIONS

Frilled curtains fitted to the back of the recess add colour and warmth to this cottage bathroom, leaving the sill free for use and disguising a poor outlook.

Project 3:
• • • • • • • • •

Creative Cover-up

Unfortunately, in every home, there is almost always at least one boring or awkward window. If this occurs in a bathroom, a fine voile ruched on to rods fitted to the window frame can be a simple solution – the light is allowed through but the view is obscured and privacy is maintained.

If a window with an ugly outlook is necessary for light, the best solution is lace curtains which will give a 'fuzzy' outline to the offending vista whilst allowing plenty of light to come into the room. There are beautiful copies of Victorian lace and embroidered panels available today at very reasonable prices, with the benefit of being machine washable. Just fit the panel on to a narrow rod and suspend it across the window. Wash it as necessary to release grime and re-hang whilst still damp to allow the fabric to stretch in situ. Alternatively, use several layers of coloured organdie to draw the attention to the light reflections rather than the view.

The most difficult situations occur where the outlook is dark and, although there is a window in the wall which must be dressed, there seems little point to it; a brick wall may have been built too close, an oil tank badly situated, or an untended hedge or large tree grown up and obscured the view. The best way to treat this situation is to dress the window as though you have chosen to cover it – but give the impression that you might open a curtain or pull a blind at any time!

I chose this treatment for a modern house which had been built at a lower level between two neighbouring houses, with a bedroom window looking right at the neighbour's garden shed wall. The fine white muslin acts as a shield against the view yet lets in light. The second 'layer' of this treatment is the blind, its line made softer by the ties. The third 'layer' is the actual curtains, lined with a fabric of the same weight and texture, but of a different pattern, for effect.

A detail of the way in which the long ties hold the fabric in place as it is rolled up to the required level.

Project 3: *Creative Cover-up*
• • • • • • • • • •

Measure the window for the main curtains from a pole 10cm (4 in) above the window frame, muslin unlined curtains from the top of the window frame to the floor, and for a flat blind.

Allow 30cm (12 in) for the headings and 12cm (4 ¾ in) for the hems.

Fit a wire for the muslin curtains against the frame of the window. Fit a narrow batten for the blind the exact width of the window to the top of the frame, and fit a wooden pole in front, 10cm (4 in) above, with the brackets to either side of the batten. The blind will never be pulled up completely so it does not matter if it is a tight fit at the top.

Materials

- fabric 1 (curtain front) as estimated
- fabric 2 (curtain lining) as estimated
  (leading edge borders) 2 pieces, 24cm (9 in) x measured length
  (blind ties) 8 pieces, 15 x 200cm (6 x 40 in)
  (blind border) 1 piece, 15cm (6 in) x measured length
- fabric 3 (blind) as estimated
- velcro
- muslin as estimated

1 To make the curtains, pin each of the two border strips to the leading edges and hems, right sides together. Fold over at the corner to make a mitre and stitch 1.5cm (⅝ in) in from the edge.

2 Press and fold towards the back, leaving a 10cm (4 in) border on the front. Herringbone stitch the raw edge to the inside of the curtain.

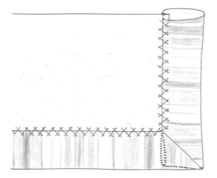

3 Place one curtain front on to the worktable, right side down. Turn in the outside edge 6cm (2 ⅜ in). Insert the weights into the corners. Ladder stitch to close, and herringbone stitch the side in place. Place the lining over. Slip stitch to the border along the side; hem exactly 10cm (4 in) from the edge and 3cm (1 ¼ in) from the outside edge.

4 Measure up from the hemline and mark the overall drop. Tack along this line. Fold over the excess fabric to give a heading of 5cm (6 in) above this line. Trim away excess and fold up 1.5cm (⅝ in). Stitch along close to the fold, and again 6cm (2 ¾ in) towards the heading, making a pocket to slip over the pole.

5 To make up the muslin curtains, allow enough widths for at least double fullness. Cut pieces to the finished length required, plus 6cm (2 ¾ in) for the hem and 8cm (3 ¼ in) for the heading. Join the widths with French seams and make 3cm (1 ¼ in) turnings on sides and hem. Slip stitch. Turn under headings 4cm (1 ½ in) double. Stitch one line close to the fold and another 2cm (¾ in) from this one, making a pocket to ruche over the rod or wires.

6 To make the blind, with right sides together, stitch the narrow border all around the sides and hem of the blind. Press to the back, press under and slip stitch to the stitching line.

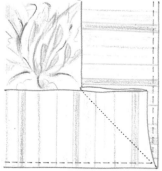

7 To make the ties, fold eight strips in half lengthways and stitch 12mm (½ in) from the outside edge and one end. Trim the corners and turn out. Press along the seam and fold line. Stitch to the top of the blind, approximately 20cm (8 in) in from the sides and at the same point front and back. Turn over 2cm (½ in) to the back. Pin Velcro over the raw edge and machine stitch in place. Staple or tack the other half of the Velcro to the batten and press together.

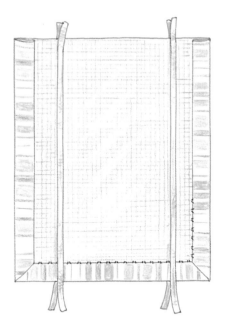

8 Make a plaited tie-back using spare pieces of all three fabrics as shown on page 23.

OTHER OPTIONS

Florals and swirls of white against a pale blue background are another interpretation of this 'cover-up' theme.

Project 4:
• • • • • • • • •
Skylight Treatment

The need for additional light in the form of a skylight can occur in any conversion or home extension where the roof space is to be incorporated. The situation can vary from the simple addition of a room in the roof space of a family home to a full-scale conversion of a building such as an agricultural barn or redundant country church into residential accommodation. Privacy is seldom the criteria for the window dressing, but insulation and light control are likely to be important factors.

Skylight window manufacturers offer ready-made roller blinds which fit into the recess and may be raised and lowered to degrees defined by either a ratchet or notch system. When the window forms part of the room, you might like to make your own roller blind in a more interesting fabric than offered by the majority of blind manufacturers. Choose a fabric that has character and is effective when flat.
The only really successful way to fit curtains to a skylight is either from a pole at the top and tied back at the bottom, or fixed to poles at the top and bottom. Either way, operating these curtains is virtually impossible unless the window is within easy reach.

This teenager's bedroom has been built into the roof space and right into the eaves of a farmhouse, with skylights added to give direct daylight on to working areas. However, the overhead mid-day sun needed to be heavily filtered to reduce the glare. A lightweight blind would have allowed too much light to enter the room during the early morning sleeping hours, so a solid blind with adjustable opening positions was designed. The star pattern gave the idea of enclosing the whole window in an interesting and individual 'frame'. To allow the window to open enough for ventilation, the 'sun' was built out 5cm (2 in) from the window frame and the blind fitted within the made-up frame rather than on the window.

Another way to treat a round window features a row of brass hooks above the window frame, and a white curtain to hook across.

Project 4: *Skylight Treatments*

Measure the window and draw to size on brown or other strong paper. Mark the opening needed and draw your design around. Cut this out on 6mm (¼ in) board. Paint or cover with fabric.

Make a simple wooden frame 5cm (2 in) deep, and fit to the outside edge of the window. Paint or cover with fabric to match.

Measure the inside of the frame accurately and deduct 6mm (¼ in) on either size for the finished width of the blind. Add 20cm (8 in) to the window length for the length of the blind. Screw the brackets which come with the kit to the inside top of the frame. You must use a spirit level and be absolutely accurate in your measurements or the blind will gradually pull to one side. It will then either rub against the woodwork and be difficult to control, or will tear and be useless.

Materials

- 1 x roller blind kit cut to your width measurement
- fabric as measurements
- framework

1 Cut the fabric to size and hang outside whilst you spray it with the stiffening solution. Leave to dry. Once completely dry, trim the sides neatly with very sharp scissors and make sure that the blind has been uniformly stiffened.

2 Fold the bottom edge under 4cm (1 ½ in) to the back and machine stitch. Cut the lath 2cm (¾ in) shorter than the blind width and insert. Screw the cord-holder to the centre of the blind through the fabric and the wood. This will prevent the lath slipping out of the pocket.

3 Tack the fabric to the guide line on the roll. This must also be very accurate to prevent the blind pulling to one side. Spring the mechanism as instructed in the kit and slot into the brackets.

NOTE: This skylight is easily reached by hand, but often they are not. If your skylight is high, extend the cord and thread through a small hole in the centre of the bottom edge of the framework. Try to find a cord which will match your wall colour and fit it to the wall as inconspicuously as possible.

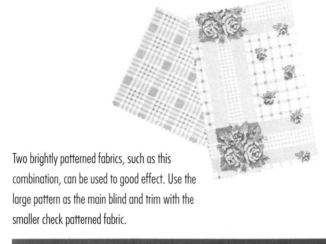

Two brightly patterned fabrics, such as this combination, can be used to good effect. Use the large pattern as the main blind and trim with the smaller check patterned fabric.

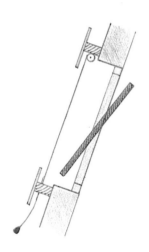

Right: The blind, open to let in the light. It looks even more effective this way, too. In this photograph, you can clearly see how the frame has been placed over the window frame.

Project 5:
· · · · · · · · · ·

Checked Curtains for a Casement Window

Casement windows are the earliest form of opening window. Usually grouped in one, two, three or four sections, with no more than two opening sections, the opening sections may swing either in or out. Most modern house windows are of casement design, as this method of construction adapts equally well to a small square window as to a large wide window. Often both window sections will open outwards.

Small casement windows need to be dressed so that fabric can be pulled back away from the window to allow as much light into the room as possible. Large, elegant casements in tall rooms look best with the drapes fitted to the frame, kept in proportion to the room.

All types of blinds may be used successfully, but the smaller the window the less complicated the design should be. Austrian and festoons must not be 'blowsy' and Roman, roller or cascade blinds should be matched to the atmosphere, whether formal or informal, of the room.

Blue and white gingham, trimmed with red buttons and red and white gingham ties, makes an attractive window treatment for a living room. The gingham is attached to a plain blue background curtain. Follow the instructions on the following pages and you, too, will be able to create this effect in your home.

This shows a detail of the way buttons and ties are attached.

Project 5: *Checked Curtains*
· · · · · · · · ·

With a little imagination, even the simplest fabrics - in this case denim and gingham - and the simplest methods, such as these unlined curtains, can be put together to make an interesting and individual window treatment.

I used a North American patchwork quilt as my inspiration. The fabrics have a good old-fashioned, tough and hardwearing feel which will combine equally well with other country fabrics, be they homespun Shaker checks and stripes and pine furniture, or bright yellows and beach-inspired colours.

Simple unlined curtains have been finished with hand-pleated headings and the two are held together with buttons and decorative ties.

A simple wooden pole was chosen for this window to suit the simplicity of the fabrics and the window itself. Decide how far your curtains need to stack back from the window to allow as much light as possible to enter; poles look best fitted 10-12cm (4-4¾ in) above the window reveal. Fit the pole (see page 24) and measure the hook drop – from the bottom of the ring to the floor and the width of the pole.

Calculate the fabric for the back curtain as shown on page 12. The top curtain will be 15cm (6 in) less than the hook drop plus headings of 2cm (¾in) and a hem of 8cm (3 ¼ in). Allow double fullness for the curtains and estimate as shown on page 12.

I used 4.2m (14 ft) of the top fabric and 4.9m (16 ft 6 in) of the under fabric.

Materials

- top fabric as estimated
- under fabric as estimated
- 1m (40 in) contrast fabric
- buttons (I used 50)
- 10cm (4 in) heading buckram as estimated
- 10 strips of gingham ribbon, each 40cm (16 in) long

1 Make the denim curtains, following the instructions for unlined curtains on page 15, leaving the heading.

2 Make the gingham curtains in the same way, making the 8cm (3 ¼ in) allowance for both sides and hem. Leave the heading.

3 To make the pleated headings, place one denim curtain on the worktable, right side up. Measure from the hem and mark the hook drop at 30cm (12 in) intervals across the width. Place the stiffened heading buckram along this line. Fold the main fabric over and under the buckram and pin.

Measure the finished flat width. Take the finished curtain width from this figure to calculate how much fabric there will be for the pleats. On our curtains, allowing five pleats and four gaps between per width of fabric, there are five pleats of 13 cm. (I will only use centimetres for our calculations to keep things simple.) Deduct the overlap and return allowance from the finished width and divide the remaining figure into four 'gaps':

63 – 8 – 10 = 45 ÷ 4 = 11.25cm.

Mark the top of the curtain with pins:

– 8 – / 13 / – 11.25 – / 13 / – 11.25 – / 13 / – 11.25 – / 13 / – 11.25 – / 13 / – 10 –

Fold the fabric inside to make the pleats. Pin and stitch down 8cm (3 ¼ in). Slip stitch the ends down to neaten and repeat with the other curtain.

4 To make the gingham top curtains, lie the fabric flat, measure and mark the finished length - hook drop less 15cm (6 in). Trim the excess fabric to 4cm (1 ¼ in), press to the wrong side, double under and hem. Fold the fabric into four at the top and mark the divisions with pins. Make pleats of 10cm (4 in) at each point and pin to the top of each of the inverted denim pleats. Secure with buttons and tie gingham ribbons around each for decoration.

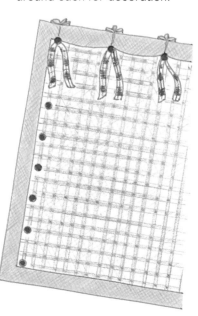

Other Ideas

- A thin metal pole would be equally effective and very convenient if there is very little room above the window.
- Covering a plain pole with either the gingham or denim fabric would also be fun in an informal setting.

OTHER OPTIONS

Scarf rings and a panel of fabric combine to create an effective window treatment for a casement window. The striped blind adds further visual interest and acts as a foil to the cold coming in through the window.

Project 6:
• • • • • • • • •

Horizontal Treatment

I have used the term horizontal to describe any window which is wider than it is long; your window may fill a whole wall or may be not much more than a slit at the top of a room which has been added for the sole purpose of increasing the available daylight in a room. Just occasionally horizontal windows are also picture windows, having been fitted to take in a panoramic view; on the whole, sadly, these windows are far less interesting, occurring in modern buildings and flats with low ceilings and very little inherent character to give atmosphere or direction to your decorations. An uninteresting window seems to lead to an opportunity for elaborate treatment to take the eye away from the structure; in practice, however, because of their proportions, horizontal windows are not very easy to dress effectively. An added problem is that there is very often a radiator positioned below, making long curtains difficult.

The room, rather than the window shape, should dictate the way these windows are dressed. If there is a stunning view, select fabrics which will not detract from the window during the daytime - you may prefer not to cover the window at all in the evening but to light the vista outside instead. If you do use curtains, they should be simple and tone with the wall colour so that there are no shocks when they are pulled; a whole wall of contrast or large bright pattern is risky and will only work in an extremely well-designed room. Blinds to filter sunlight may be needed. Use vertical blinds or a roller blind in a neutral colour which will pull out of the way on a dull day.

simply tack the drape to the top of the board with thumb tacks. The curtains can be ruched over a smaller pole fitted behind the drapery pole, or hooked to a narrow, lightweight track fitted behind the pole.

Either scoop these curtains up to either side of the radiator at night, to allow the heat through, or fit a blind behind the drape - a rolled blind would be a complementary treatment.

Measure the window as shown for the length of curtains and the drape. One width of fabric will be enough for a small window but a large window should have two or more widths joined. Calculate heading allowance to gather with a tape if fitted to a track, or to ruche over the pole is using double poles.

Horizontal windows are typical of '60s and '70s architecture. Radiators were almost always fitted directly below the window, making elegant window treatments very difficult. The treatment here is very simple to make yet extremely effective, and can be

adapted to any room and any size and shape of window.

I have used a simple metal pole for the drape. You may prefer brass, or might like to cover your pole with fabric, or to paint it. If you already have a pelmet board fitted, make use of it;

A loosely draped sari makes an elegant curtain treatment for a plain window with a radiator placed underneath it. The sari drapes to either side, leaving the window sill space available for displaying personal treasures.

Project 6: *Horizontal Treatment*

Materials

- main fabric (I used 2 sari lengths) as estimated for drape
- pole or pelmet board
- fabric for sash tie, 1.5m (62 in)
- 2 tie-back hooks

1 To make the curtains, cut the sari into lengths as estimated. Allow an extra 15-20cm (6-8 in) to let the curtains bump on to the floor. Join the widths with French seams. Turn the sides under with a 2.5cm (1 in) double hem and slip stitch invisibly. Turn the hem up with a 6 cm (2 ⅜ in) double hem or adjust to suit the sari pattern. Slip stitch as before. Measure from the hem to your finished drop and fold the heading allowance to the wrong side. Either stitch a pocket to accommodate the pole or stitch the heading tape in place 6 cm (2⅜ in) down.

2 To make the drape, neaten the cut ends of the sari. Press 5cm (2 in) to the wrong side all around. Fold under to make 'hems' of 2.5cm (I in). Pin, press and stitch. You might like to machine stitch this with a decorative stitch in the darkest colour or, if you have embroidery skills, use them to make an attractive feather-stitched edge.

3 Now fit the drape: stand on a ladder and start from one side, with the fabric slightly draping on the floor. Fold the drape over and over, keeping the right side to the front. The folds will need to be as first measured or you will either run out of fabric or have too much at the other side. Keep adjusting until you are happy with the result. Secure in several places with thumb tacks into the pole. Remember to remove these tacks before taking the drape down for cleaning.

4 If you would like to hold the cutains back, make a sash to hold the draped sides. Cut a piece of fabric 60cm (24 in) wide and 1.5m (62 in) long. Fold in half lengthways, right sides together. Cut each end away at an angle of 45 degrees. Stitch from each end to within 6cm (2 ⅜ in) of the centre. Snip across each point, close to the stitches. Turn right sides out, using a pin to make sharp corners. Press along the seam and slip stitch the gap. Using double thread, gather the centre together and stitch a small brass ring to the fabric. Secure. Slip this over the tie-back hook and tie a knot or bow to hold the side drapes.

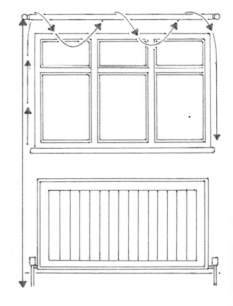

OTHER OPTIONS

Using two different saris, in contrasting colours, you can make a softly elegant curtain for a window where you still wish to let the light in, but need to maintain a certain level of privacy. Left: Try this colour combintation for a different effect.

Project 7:
• • • • • • • • • •
French Dressing

French windows finish at the floor and may open either inwards or outwards, planned with the sole purpose of allowing access to the outside from rooms or corridors which adjoin a garden, courtyard or patio. These outside areas become outdoor rooms and an extension of normal family living for several months of the year, so any window treatment must address the problem of through traffic.

This style of window offers fairly limited scope for elaborate dressing. Curtains must be suitable for catching or pulling back well away from the opening doors, and cannot be draped over the doorway. Pelmets need to finish high enough to allow the doors to open, especially if they open inwards, so design is again restricted.

Silk linen curtains, bound all around with yellow ochre, look marvellous against the wood frames and the courtyard beyond. They have been made with very little fullness to allow them to be pulled back into restricted space but have been interlined with a lightweight woven cotton to add extra body, with the added advantage of providing some insulation and draught- proofing in the winter months. The same fabric is used front and back. Almost any type of pole could have been used - dark or light wood, painted or brass. I used a narrow piece of black iron rod with simple curtain rings. I made sash tie-backs (page 21), which can be tied either high or low to keep the curtains from floating out in a summer breeze.

A billowing sheer fabric curtain ensures privacy when pulled across the French doors in this living room. When people need to go in and out of the door, the curtain is pulled to one side.

Project 7: *French Dressing*
· · · · · · · · · ·

Fit your pole just above the window and as far to the side as needed for clearance. Measure from the bottom of the curtain ring to the floor. Add 15cm (6 in) to make the curtains over-long and 40cm (16 in) - approximately one-fifth of the drop - for the attached pelmet. This hook drop was 215cm (7 ft 2 in), so the cut length was 270cm (9 ft).

These curtains have one-and-a-half times fullness of fabric, so measure the curtain pole, multiply by one-and-a-half and divide by the width of your fabric. This window required three widths, so one-and-a-half widths in each curtain for both front and back .

The contrast binding will be cut to go all around the curtains and should be 12cm (4 ¾ in) wide.

Materials

- main fabric as estimated
- interlining or a thick cotton fabric, same quantity as main fabric
- contrast binding fabric as estimated
- heading web, 3 widths
- pole and curtain hooks

1 Cut the six lengths and join into four, with one and a half widths in each, using flat seams. Cut and join the three pieces of interlining in the same way. Press. Place the interlining on your worktable and press to remove any creases. Lay one piece of the main fabric over, right side up, and press. Fold the main fabric back and lock stitch to the interlining on the seam and half way across the full width. Smooth the main fabric flat over the interlining and pin all around. Trim the interlining to fit the main fabric exactly.

2 Cut out strips of the binding fabric 12cm (4 ¾ in) wide to go all around the curtain. You will need to join the strips on the cross so that when the fabric is folded over the bulk is reduced. Press seams.

3 Pin the binding all around, with the pins placed 3cm (1 ¼ in) from the outside edges. Fold the binding over at right angles at each corner and pin as far as the fold.

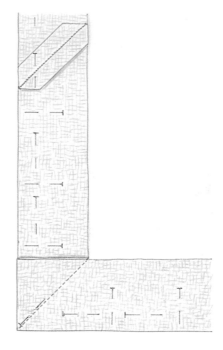

4 Machine stitch the binding following exactly the 3cm (1 ¼ in) line. As you reach the fold in each corner, stop, back stitch, lift the needle, fold the flap over and start again on the other side. Press the binding away from the main fabric.

5 Place the curtain back on to your worktable, right side down. Lie another curtain piece over, matching seams, fold back and lock in as before. Trim if necessary to line up with the interlining on all four sides. Press the binding towards the back and fold under to leave 3cm (1 ¼ in) showing. At each corner snip, 3cm (1 ¼ in) as shown and fold back in a natural mitre.

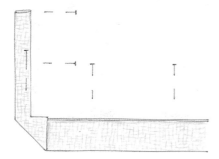

OTHER OPTIONS

6 Measure from the top, 40cm (16 in). Pin the heading tape along this line so that the 'pelmet' remains 40cm (16 in) long and stitch through all layers. Fold the pelmet to the front and stitch the five hooks at even distances along the width.

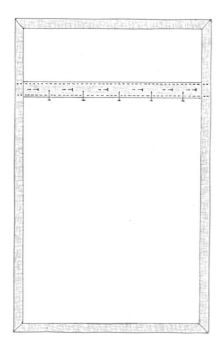

This French window opens onto a small patio and is frequently open in the summer. In this situation, the sheer fabric is draped to one side and held with a *passementerie* tie-back. Right: Try this colour combination for a different effect.

Project 8:
· · · · · · · · ·
Sash Style

Almost any window treatment is possible on a sash window as it is rare to find one which goes against the size and proportion of the room in which it is fitted. Some interior designers choose Austrian or festoon blinds but you may prefer to dress a long, tall sash window with curtains. A curtain designed in conjunction with a pelmet is an excellent idea. The purpose of the pelmet is to lower the eye level. There are many ideas for covering a wooden pelmet: try padding, adding long fringing, and quilting a piece of fabric are just three you may like to consider. Blind and curtain combinations also work well. A blind left two-thirds down will make a narrow window seem wider and will be more pleasing to the eye. Used with a curtain, it could appear quite lavish.

Alternatively, fixed headings with the curtains tied back at a height of one-third from the floor give shape to sash windows. Double- or multi-layer curtains can create a great effect, with each layer pulled back at a different height from the floor. The final effect will be of fabric cascading from the top to the floor. Period houses are frequently altered internally to add an extra bathroom or bedroom and this sometimes results in the window of the existing room being divided to give light to the added room. Usually the major part of the window will have been left with the larger room and the 'borrowed' window will be very narrow for its height. A blind left two-thirds down helps to redress this imbalance and is pleasing to the eye.

I wanted a bright Mediterranean feel for this second-floor, city bedroom, which, although not directly overlooked, does have houses opposite and can sometimes feel a little closed in. Off-white walls and wood floors combine perfectly with the strong blues of the curtain fabric to give a fresh, open atmosphere. The simple stripe used on the front of the curtains gives way to the pretty but strong Provençal-pattern lining when the curtains are hooked back. The fixed heading was chosen to make the most of the contrast lining and, at the same time, block out some of the buildings opposite.

This shows a detail of the scalloped edge, revealing the lining.

Project 8: *Sash Style*
• • • • • • • • • •

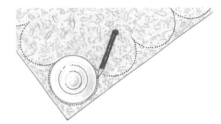

Materials

- fabric 1 (front) as estimated
- fabric 2 (lining) as estimated
- embroidery thread (I used 2 skeins)
- embroidery needle
- heading tape (I used dainty tape)
- Velcro
- heading buckram or strong paper for making the template

For this treatment , it is best to choose your lining fabric first and then select a complementary small check or stripe for the front.

Scalloped headings, hems and sides were made and then blanket-stitched in the darkest tone of blue for simple, effective

detail. This lovely soft finish is well worth the extra time but, if you feel unable to tackle this yet, buy a narrow ribbon and stitch it just inside the edge before you put the lining and main fabric together.

Measure your window and estimate fabric as shown on page 10-12.

Cut a batten 5cm (2 in) deep, and the width of the window. Cover in fabric and fit to the frame. Fit tie-back hooks approximately two-thirds up from the floor.

This window was 125cm (50 in) wide and the top of the frame was 230cm (7 ft 8 in) from the floor. I allowed nothing for headings and hems except a cutting tolerance of 5cm (2 in). One width of fabric gave just over double fullness to this window.

1 Using a small saucer, a wine glass or compasses, make a scalloped template for the curtain sides. With the front fabric right side down on the worktable, start at the outside edge and draw around the scallops along the heading, the leading edge and the hem. At the top and bottom corners, make a larger circle to accommodate the turns.

2 Place both fabrics together, right sides inwards, and pin all around both inside and outside the marked scallops. Stitch carefully, following the drawn line. Trim to within 6mm (¼ in) all around, snipping tight into the points.

3 Turn right sides out and press the scallops flat. Fold under both sides of the outer edge and slip stitch together.

4 Stitch heading tape to the wrong side.

5 Make blanket stitches all
around, approximately 12mm
(½ in) long and apart - choose a
larger stitch for a busy pattern or
strong colours or a smaller stitch
for softer colours or a small
pattern.

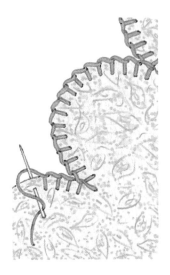

6 Pull the heading tape up to
half of the batten size and
stitch Velcro to hold the gathers in
place.

7 Fit the curtain up and drape
the leading edge to the tie-
back to find a pleasing shape.
Mark this position. Make two small
tabs by rolling narrow pieces of
fabric; cut two stitches in the
seam, insert the tabs and stitch
very neatly and thoroughly.

OTHER OPTIONS

This sash window features a roll-up patterned fabric
blind held up with a soft bow, with a sheer fabric
draped across the top of the window. The white
fabric creates a romantic look as it falls to the floor,
where it has been allowed to rest neatly.

A collection of red and gold patterned fabrics would
also look wonderful when made up into this curtain
design. This is a traditional and regal look.

Project 9:
• • • • • • • • •

Across the Arch

Arched windows, whether large or small, new or old, are always an important architectural feature of the house and will have been planned primarily for the external elevation, often placed above the front entrance of the main facade giving light inside on a stairway or landing. They may be from floor to ceiling or from a low sill, usually in a major room and always with a view.

You may be unfortunate enough to have a lovely arched window with either no view at all or one which needs to be minimised. An attractive and practical answer to this problem is to make permanent curtaining in a light muslin or organdie which will filter the view whilst still allowing the structure of the window to be seen; fullness of fabric will hide the view more successfully but allow less light in, while a little fullness will just soften the outlook. White sheers will allow the most light through, but interesting effects can be achieved by using coloured muslins or even layers of fabric in varying colours. Try using pale lemon, white and the softest pink together, or lilac, soft green and soft blue. Stencilled designs on pale colours also add interest and a personalised style. Several layers may be built up and hung together.

These permanent drapes can be fitted on to hooks, tacked to the window frame, or hooked to a special track. It is possible to buy tracks which are manufactured in small sections to fit any arched shape, allowing curtains to be hung within the frame of the window.

This is the same sheer fabric without the sari draped across the top of the arch. The fabric has been stencilled with a fleur de lys design, which can easily be done at home using a cardboard stencil and a can of stencil paint.

This treatment has been designed to fit any width of arched window or arched doorway, whether of little or great architectural merit. The lower drape can be lifted or drawn back when privacy is not required. The top is decorated in more detail and acts as a complete block to prying eyes.

Project 9: *Across the Arch*
• • • • • • • • • •

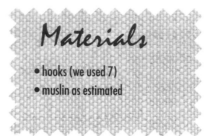

Materials

• hooks (we used 7)
• muslin as estimated

To estimate your fabric, multiply the arch width by three and divide by the width of the fabric. Measure from the top of the arch to the floor and add 20cm (8 in) for each length. Allow one width of fabric for the top drape to go over the arch, plus one metre (one yard) on either side.

For a very easy fixing, we have fitted small cupped hooks to the outside edge of the frame at approximately 30cm (12 in) intervals. An alternative might be wooden pegs, stained or painted.

For an arched opening, either fit a small batten around the edge so that the curtain may be tacked into it or a track fitted to the wood, or just fit the hooks into the ceiling.

1 Cut the piece of muslin fabric into two and join to make one wide curtain piece. Use French seams and stitch half widths to either side of a full width to avoid an ugly centre seam. Press seams lightly. Turn over 5cm (2 in) on both sides. Press, fold this in half to make turnings measuring 2.5cm (1 in) and pin. Repeat with the hem and header using a width of 10cm (4 in), folded to 5cm (2 in). Slip-stitch or machine stitch around all sides of the fabric.

2 To attach to the arched window: Screw brass hooks into the frame, beginning with the centre top. Place one on each side of the frame at points 2 and 3 in the illustration. Then add hooks to points 4, 5, 6 and 7. We used net curtain clasps to attach the fabric to the brass hooks.

3 Divide the muslin into the number of spaces between hooks. In this case, six. Mark the top of each section with pins or marking tacks. Take the centre of the fabric and attach it to the centre brass hook. Let the fabric fall to the floor. Attach the side edges to points 2 and 3 so that

the hemline is touching the floor, or dropping onto the floor to the same amount of fabric as below the first hook. Let the top fall towards the front. Adjust the fabric as you attach it to points 4, 5, 6 and 7, keeping the hemline level and letting the heading fall into even scallops. You may prefer to decorate the top edge of the heading with stitching or trim with a ribbon.

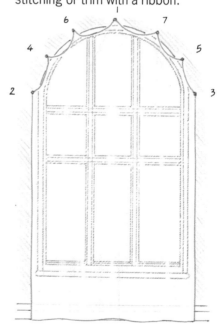

Other Ideas

An interesting alternative to this treatment could be to use a black metal pole, specially shaped and fitted to the edge of the frame. Take a template of the arch to a local ironmonger and ask him to bend a steel rod to your shape, adding rings or nibs at approximately 30cm (12 in) intervals to tie or hook the drape. Paint the pole a suitable colour using metal paint.

Stitch Guide

Buttonhole stitch

Working from left to right, push the needle up through the fabric, pointing away from the edge. Twist the thread around the point and pull the needle through. Keep the threads as straight as possible and pull so that a knot forms on the edge of the fabric.

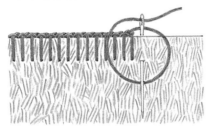

Hemming stitch

Used on the hems of lined curtains and the hems and sides of unlined curtains. Slide the needle through the folded hem for 1.5cm (½ in). Pick up two threads of the main fabric and push needle back into the fold immediately. Slide through 1.5cm (½ in) and continue.

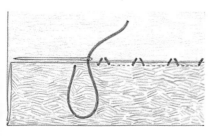

Herringbone stitch

Working from left to right (for right handers) the needle should always be used from right to left. Stitch into the wrong side of the main fabric, picking up two threads. Approx. 1.5cm (½ in) to the right and 1.5cm (½ in) down make a stitch into the hem. Pull through and stitch again into the wrong side

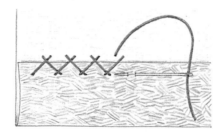

Ladder stitch

Used to join two folds together. Slide needle along fold 0.5cm (⅛ in) and straight into the fold opposite. Slide along for 0.5cm (⅛ in) and straight into the fold opposite. Slide along for 0.5cm (⅛ in) and back into the first fold again directly opposite.

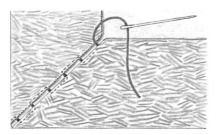

Locking in stitch

Used to hold lining to main fabric so that the fabrics cannot separate but allowing each fabric some degree of movement. Always use the same colour thread as the main fabric. Fold back the lining, secure thread to the lining and make a small stitch in the main fabric just below. Make a large loop 10cm (4 in) long and make a small stitch in the lining inside this loop. Stitch into the main fabric. Allow the stitch to remain slightly loose.

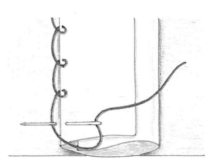

Long stitch

Used to hold the sides of interlined curtains. It measures approx. 1cm (¼ in) across and 4cm (1½ in) long on the diagonal.

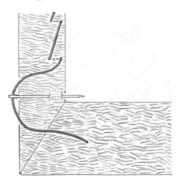

Slip stitch

Slide the needle through the main fabric 1.5cm (½ in). Pick up two threads of the lining. Push needle back into the main fabric exactly opposite and slide through 1.5cm (½ in).

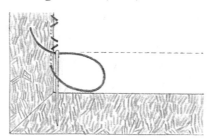

Pinning

When pinning two layers of fabric together or pinning piping on to fabric, always use horizontal and vertical pins to keep the fabric in place from both directions. The horizontal pins need to be removed just before the machine foot reaches them; the vertical ones can remain in place so the fabrics are held together the whole time.

Index